First World War
and Army of Occupation
War Diary
France, Belgium and Germany

36 DIVISION
Divisional Troops
Service Squadron 6 Inniskilling Dragoons
5 October 1915 - 30 May 1916

WO95/2496/1

The Naval & Military Press Ltd
www.nmarchive.com
Published in association with The National Archives

Published by

The Naval & Military Press Ltd

Unit 10 Ridgewood Industrial Park,

Uckfield, East Sussex,

TN22 5QE England

Tel: +44 (0) 1825 749494

www.naval-military-press.com

www.nmarchive.com

This diary has been reprinted in facsimile from the original. Any imperfections are inevitably reproduced and the quality may fall short of modern type and cartographic standards.

© **Crown Copyright**
Images reproduced by permission of The National Archives, London, England, 2015.

Contents

Document type	Place/Title	Date From	Date To
Heading	WO95/2496/1		
Heading	36th Division Divl Troops 1st Soon 6th Innis Dragoons Oct 1915-May 1916 To 10 Corps.		
Heading	36th Division 1st S. Squad 6th Corps Vol 1 121/7708 Oct 15 May 16		
War Diary	Bordon	05/10/1915	05/10/1915
War Diary	Le Harve	06/10/1915	06/10/1915
War Diary	Amiens	07/10/1915	07/10/1915
War Diary	Olincourt	09/10/1915	22/10/1915
War Diary	St. Hilaire	23/10/1915	28/10/1915
Heading	36th Division 1st S. Squad 6th Dgns Vol 2		
War Diary	St. Hilaire	02/11/1915	28/11/1915
Heading	36th 1st S. Sq. 6th Inniskg Dgns Vol 3		
Miscellaneous	War Diary of Service Squadron VI Inniskilling Dragoons From 1st December 1915 To 31st December 1915 Volume III		
War Diary	Famechon Ref. Map Amiens 1.80.000	01/12/1915	04/12/1915
War Diary	Famechon	05/12/1915	31/12/1915
Heading	36 1st S. Sq. 6th Inniskg Dgns. Vol: 4		
Heading	War Diary of Service Squadron 6th Inniskilling Dragoons From 1st January 1916 To 31st January 1916 Volume IV		
War Diary	Famechon	01/01/1916	03/01/1916
War Diary	St. Hilaire	04/01/1916	31/01/1916
Heading	War Diary of Service Squadron 6th Inniskilling Dragoons From 1st February 1916 To 31st March 1916		
Heading	War Diary Of Service Squadron 6th Inniskilling Dragoons From 1st February 1916 To 29th February 1916 Volume V		
War Diary	St. Hilaire	09/02/1916	09/02/1916
War Diary	Lavicogne	22/02/1916	22/02/1916
Heading	War Diary of Service Squadron 6th Inniskilling Dragoons From 1st March 1916 To 31st March 1916 Volume VI		
War Diary	Vauchelles	04/03/1916	04/03/1916
War Diary	Bertrancourt	04/03/1916	04/03/1916
Heading	War Diary of 6th Inniskilling Dragoons (Service Squadron) From 1st March 1916 To 31st March 1916 Volume 6		
Heading	War Diary of Service Squadron 6th Inniskilling Dragoons From 1st March 1916 To 31st March 1916 Volume VI		
War Diary	Vauchelles Les Authie	01/03/1916	01/03/1916
War Diary	Bertrancourt	01/03/1916	25/03/1916
Heading	War Diary of Service Squadron 6th Inniskilling Dragoons From 1st April 1916 To 30th April 1916		
Heading	War Diary of Service Squadron 6th Inniskilling Dragoons From 1st April 1916 To 30th April 1916 Volume VII		
War Diary	Contay	01/04/1916	04/04/1916

War Diary	St. Ouen	07/04/1916	07/04/1916
War Diary	St. Riquier	13/04/1916	13/04/1916
War Diary	Martainne Ville	20/04/1916	25/04/1916
War Diary	Hangest	26/04/1916	26/04/1916
War Diary	Sur-Somme	27/04/1916	27/04/1916
War Diary	Puchevillers	28/04/1916	28/04/1916
Heading	War Diary of Service Squadron 6th Inniskilling Dragoons From 1st May 1916 To 31st May 1916 Volume VIII		
War Diary	Pochvillers	01/05/1916	30/05/1916

WO 95/24961

36TH DIVISION
DIVL TROOPS

1ST SQDN 6TH INNIS DRAGOONS
OCT 1915 – MAY 1916

To 10 Corps

36th Kurscum

1st S. Squad: 6th & 8 gns:
tot I

121/7408

Oct 15
Nov 16

Army Form C. 2118.

Original

WAR DIARY
~~INTELLIGENCE SUMMARY~~

(Erase heading not required.)

Instructions regarding War Diaries and Intelligence Summaries are contained in F. S. Regs., Part II. and the Staff Manual respectively. Title pages will be prepared in manuscript.

Place	Date	Hour	Summary of Events and Information	Remarks and references to Appendices
London	5.X.5.14		Strength of Squadron leaving England — 5 officers 146 other ranks 161 horses 2 Maxim machine guns 3 G.S. waggons 1 cook's cart under command of Capt A. Churchill. The Service Squadron. O. Remobilising waggon left Roton camp in two trains at 11.0 am & 12.30 pm arrived at Southampton at 3 pm & 5 pm. The men horses were embarked on board the transports "City of Chester" The transport sailed at 5 pm that evening and arrived at the Port of Le Havre next morning without mishap.	Capt A Churchill 2/L
Le Havre	6.X.14		Squadron disembarked the day and remained on the wharf at the Port till 4 pm. From there were marched thro' the streets to the railway station and entrained the troop train left and all on train at 9 pm.	"
Amiens	7.X.14		Squadron arrived by train at & Amiens siding outside Amiens at 7.15 am. Detrained and marched thro' town to bivouacs and proceeded to bivs at Glincourt.	"
Glincourt	8.X.14		Amiens S. Belgium reported the armed ambulances to the Amiens.	
Glincourt	12.X.14		Instructions of the Squadron by the divisional commander Major McGuire Capt Michie Regt Quinn left to attend a Gunnery class.	"
Glincourt	12.X.14			"

Army Form C. 2118.

WAR DIARY
or
INTELLIGENCE SUMMARY.
(Erase heading not required.)

Instructions regarding War Diaries and Intelligence Summaries are contained in F.S. Regs., Part II. and the Staff Manual respectively. Title pages will be prepared in manuscript.

Place	Date	Hour	Summary of Events and Information	Remarks and references to Appendices
Olincourt	19th Nov		M⁴ Hutchins left in charge of details at Boulogne reported his arrival at Olincourt	
Olincourt	19.11.15		Capt Miller Reg¹ Quarter-master joined to effect the carrying of training	
Olincourt	19.11.15		Tactical scheme in conjunction with 1st Indian Cavalry Corps Re.	
			Division acted as Armoured Guard and after completion of this	"
			duty joined the Regiment of the Ferozeshah Brigade and	"
			worked under the direction of Col. Patterson for the remainder	"
			of the day.	"
			Capt Miller per troop delivered as ambulance orderlies under the instruction	" Mr
			of Staff Officer.	
Olincourt	21.11.15		Tactical scheme with Meerut Division.	"
Olincourt	22.11.15		Squadron left Olincourt by route march to new billets at	"
			S¹ Hilaire. All horses and men arrived here.	
S¹ Hilaire	23. Nov		Thick rain prohibited calling the attention of all ranks	
			to the importance of paying proper compliments to our allies.	
S¹ Hilaire	25.11.15		The Motor Division marched 7½ miles VERT GALAND and on	Weather
			drawing up on the W side of road running N.S. BEAUVAL the squadron	foggy
			formed up in line with the R.F.A. ⇒ on its left and the 36ᵗʰ Cyclists Coy.	

1577 Wt. W10791/1773 500,000 1/15 D.D.&L. A.D.S.S./Forms/C. 2118.

Army Form C. 2118.

WAR DIARY
or
INTELLIGENCE SUMMARY.
(Erase heading not required.)

Instructions regarding War Diaries and Intelligence Summaries are contained in F. S. Regs., Part II. and the Staff Manual respectively. Title pages will be prepared in manuscript.

Place	Date	Hour	Summary of Events and Information	Remarks and references to Appendices
St Hilaire	2nd Dec		Yesterday on its right the Majesty the King George accompanied by the French President drove along the front of the Western Division in an open car at 3.40 pm.	
St Hilaire	3rd		Official order drawing attention to the distinctive badges of the officers in the French Army.	
St Hilaire	4th		Concert for the troops at U.21 A.9.2.5 MONTRÉT-en-FONTTIEU at 6.30 pm.	
St Hilaire 5–7th			The usual squadron and troop training.	

C Churchill Oxepholyt
Cmdg:
Service Sqdn. 5th. Dragoons.

Sgt S. Steeds, 6th Bgds
Fob 2

D/
7708

36th Kuraun

Nov 15

Army Form C. 2118.

WAR DIARY
or
INTELLIGENCE SUMMARY
(Erase heading not required.)

Instructions regarding War Diaries and Intelligence Summaries are contained in F. S. Regs., Part II. and the Staff Manual respectively. Title pages will be prepared in manuscript.

Place	Date	Hour	Summary of Events and Information	Remarks and references to Appendices
St Silvain	2.XI.15		Tactical Reserve with Observation Numordered to be very week	
"	3.XI.15		issued this night by the Divisional Commander. Special Orders issued in Cerulation of Officers	weather fine
"	4.XI.15		Tactical Reserve in conjunction with 36th Cyclist Coy	"
"	6.XI.15		A Musketry competition was commenced for the purpose of testing Section Commanders.	
"	8.XI.15		Completion of Musketry competition which was won by Corpl Reid Section with score of 280 o/o	
"	10.XI.15		Tactical exercise in conjunction with 36th Cycled Coy	
"	15.XI.15		Inspection of Horses and Bicycles by the Divisional Commander.	
"	16.XI.15		Sergt McKeown sentenced by F.G.C.M. to be reduced to the ranks and undergo No 1 Field Punishment for two months	
			Crime — Drunkenness.	
"	18.XI.15		Promotions — Actg/Corpl Kapff to be Lance Corpl vice No 133 L/Cpl Lockhart promoted Corpl. No 7 Pte Reeves to actg Lc/Cpl. No 121 Pte E. Percy to be actg Lce/Corpl.	

WAR DIARY
or
INTELLIGENCE SUMMARY

Army Form C. 2118.

Place	Date	Hour	Summary of Events and Information	Remarks and references to Appendices
St Hilaire	17.11.15		No 93 L/Sergt Newell to be L/Sergt vice No 203 Pte McKeown reduced to private. No 97 L/Corpl G.C. Reid to be L/Sergt vice J. Newell promoted. No 133 L/Corpl Lockhart to be L/Corpl vice L/Corpl Reid promoted to L/Sergt.	
"	18.11.15		The Squadron moved from St HILAIRE to new Billets at FAMECHON. The whole of the month spent at ST HILAIRE was devoted to training and improving the sanitary conditions of the billets. The weather except for a few fine days was not good and a great deal of snow & frost was experienced.	

C Chamberlayne
Cmdg.
Service Sqdn. 6th Dragoons.

1st L Sp: 6th Innisks P of Wo:
vol 3
Dec

364

Army Form C. 2118.

WAR DIARY
or
INTELLIGENCE SUMMARY.
(Erase heading not required.)

Instructions regarding War Diaries and Intelligence Summaries are contained in F. S. Regs., Part II. and the Staff Manual respectively. Title pages will be prepared in manuscript.

Place	Date	Hour	Summary of Events and Information	Remarks and references to Appendices
			CONFIDENTIAL

WAR DIARY

of

Service Squadron VI Inniskilling Dragoons

From 1st December 1915 To 31st December 1915.

VOLUME III | Kept by:- A. Hulse Capt. Service Squadron 6th Innis. Dragoons |

1577 Wt.W10791/1773 500,000 1/15 D. D. & L.   A.D.S.S./Forms/C. 2118.

Army Form C. 2118.

WAR DIARY
or
INTELLIGENCE SUMMARY.
(Erase heading not required.)

Instructions regarding War Diaries and Intelligence Summaries are contained in F.S. Regs., Part II. and the Staff Manual respectively. Title pages will be prepared in manuscript.

Place	Date	Hour	Summary of Events and Information	Remarks and references to Appendices
FAMECHON	1-12-15		The Squadron has been billeted in a small village named FAMECHON. Men are accommodated in farm buildings and all the horses under cover. A great deal of work during the next few days will be necessary to put the billets in a good state of sanitation. We are in the area of the 12th Infantry Brigade and on our left have the 2nd Batt Essex Regt billeted in the town of AILLY-LES-HAUT-CLOCHER and on our right the 14th Batt R.I. Rifles at ERGNIES and CORENFLOS. Weather wet and cold.	REF MAP AMIENS 1.80,000
REF MAP AMIENS 1.80,000			Ref map AMIENS 1.80,000	
ditto	2-12-15		Ref 3rd Army R.O. No 168. An order was published warning all ranks that shooting of game, snaring hares and rabbits is strictly prohibited. Horse exercise and men employed cleaning up billets etc. A competition to be held to appoint 6 Squadron sniper who will be issued with optical sights (Bennett Water Sight). Weather wet.	Ref. 3 Army R.O. No 188
				Ref. Sqd Order No 49
ditto	3-12-15		Order published that all transport vehicles to be washed daily and the wheels re greased. Weather rain but stormy.	36th M.O. No 57
ditto	4-12-15		Mounted Parade 8-30 am. NOTE. It has been found that with the exception of road patrols, no work over the country can be carried out owing to the heavy rain and the cultivation of crops. Weather wet.	

Army Form C. 2118.

WAR DIARY
or
INTELLIGENCE SUMMARY.
(Erase heading not required.)

Place	Date	Hour	Summary of Events and Information	Remarks and references to Appendices
FAMECHON	5-12-15	8-45 am	Church of England Parade for Divine Service at FAMECHON. Methodists and Presbyterians at 11-10 am at FAMECHON. Weather fine in the morning.	Ref. map AMIENS 1.80,000
ditto	6-12-15		Capt. R Chamberlayne detailed as member of a General Court Martial assembling at 11 am today at H.Qrs. 12th Infantry Brigade HILLY-LES-HAUT-CLOCHER. Weather Wet.	" "
		6-30 am	Mounted Parade at 6-30 am under Troop Leaders	
		2-15 pm	Physical Training + Bayonet Fighting. One copy of Sheet 11 ABBEVILLE was issued today to Troop Leaders	
ditto	7-12-15	6-30	Mounted Parade at 6-30 am under Capt. Huhn. 12-30 pm Horse Inspection 5-30 Gas Helmet Drill for N.C.I. Troops & Recreation Room 9 pm Musketry Competition. Weather Wet	
ditto	8-12-15	6-30	Horses exercised. 9 pm Musketry Competition. Weather fair. 5-30 Gas Helmet Drill. A pamphlet on defensive measures against Gas attacks will be read by Capt. Huhn	
ditto	9-12-15	9-30	Mounted Parade under R. Seymour. Inspection by Medical Officer at 2 pm. Gas Helmet Drill at 5-30 pm. Weather Fair	
ditto	10-12-15		Order published that no grenades are now to be thrown near the heads of men in trenches from a point behind the scenes thrown will only throw dummies This refers to training of Grenadiers. Weather Wet	Ref. 36.Vide 2nd Sept letter A.C.S. 8/22 6

A.M.

Army Form C. 2118.

WAR DIARY
or
INTELLIGENCE SUMMARY.
(Erase heading not required.)

Place	Date	Hour	Summary of Events and Information	Remarks and references to Appendices
FAMECHON	10-12-15			Ref. 36.10.0. No. 10 et. Ref MAP. AMIENS 1.80,000
	6-3-16		Cafe de la Place ERGNIES is placed out of bounds to all troops from 8-12-15. An arrangement has been made whereby men may have hot-baths on Wednesdays Thursdays Fridays and Saturdays. It has also been found possible to get women to wash and mend the men's clothes (under linen) and this is now being carried out weekly, which greatly adds to the comfort of men and is a preventative against vermin and scabies. Provisory frame shot-hots baths are regularly obtainable. Weather wet. The Recreation Room is in full swing now and writing pads and papers have been printed.	
Ditto	11-12-15	8.30	Mounted parade at 8.30 am under Capt. Hodson in conjunction with the 26th Div Cyclist Coy. The two forces met at the underpass but operation had to be cancelled owing to stormy weather. It has been arranged to hold an inspection each week of all harness, saddlery, rifles, swords, revolvers, ammunition, field dressings & Iodine Ampoules and Gas Helmets. A day has been allotted to each troop for these inspections to be thoroughly carried out. Weather continues wet.	

WAR DIARY
INTELLIGENCE SUMMARY

Army Form C. 2118.

Place	Date	Hour	Summary of Events and Information	Remarks and references to Appendices
FAMECHON	12-12-15		Parade for Divine Service at 8.45 am for Church of England, Presbyterians and Methodists at 9-20. The Services were held at FAMECHON. Cape National, AILLY-LES-HAUT-CLOCHER is placed out of bounds to all troops from 16-12-15 to 10-3-16. Weather fine.	Ref. Maps Amiens 1-80,000. 1st. & 2nd. Wds. Rb. No. 187 Ref. B.R.O. No. 1302.
	13-12-15		Mounted Parade at 8.45 am. Order published as follows:- There is no objection to the following being written on F.S. Postcards. "A Merry Xmas and a Happy New Year". Weather fine.	
	14-12-15		Mounted Parade at 9.30 am. General fatigue cleaning up billets. Inspection of billets by the A.D.M.S. 36th Division into supposed two satisfaction at the sanitary arrangements and the comforts for men. Weather fine.	
	15-12-15		Mounted Parade 8.45 am. Medical Inspection at 2 pm. Another mounted competition was ordered that had to be cancelled abandoned owing to the inclemency of the weather.	
	16-12-15		Mounted Parade 8.45 am. Weather wet.	

WAR DIARY or INTELLIGENCE SUMMARY

Army Form C. 2118.

(Erase heading not required.)

Instructions regarding War Diaries and Intelligence Summaries are contained in F. S. Regs., Part II. and the Staff Manual respectively. Title pages will be prepared in manuscript.

Place	Date	Hour	Summary of Events and Information	Remarks and references to Appendices
TAMÉCHON	17-12-15	10am	Inspection of train at 10 am. Musketry competition 2-15pm. Weather wet.	Ref: Map AMIENS 1-50,000
	18-12-15	8.30	Horses exercised. Musketry competition 2-15pm. Weather fine.	
	19-12-15	8.40	Church of England parade. Presbyterians & Wesleyans at 9-20am. The following men are appointed Snipers and will train under Capt Drake — Ptes Armstrong, Connor, Robinson, Williamson, Campbell, Gunn. Weather fair.	
	20-12-15	9.30	Bombing under Capt Drake at PONT REMY. Weather wet.	Ref: Map AMIENS 1-80,000
	21-12-15	8.30	Bombing. Bayonet fighting with gas helmets. 9-40 Horses exercised. Orders published warning all ranks to be in their billets by 6-30 pm. Weather wet.	
			Order published that all Cafés & Estaminets in towns or villages where troops are billeted will be closed to the troops except between the hours of 11am to 1pm - 6pm to 8pm. The purchase of spirits of any kind at Cafés or Estaminets on other Services is forbidden. M.O. Parade 8-30 am. Weather fair.	Ref: Sp. Order No. 109 22/12/15
	22-12-15		A present of Plum Puddings was received from ladies & gentlemen living in J. FERMANAGH IRELAND. The Puddings were collected forwarded to the Squadron by Mr Copeland Trimble ENNISKILLEN. A letter conveying the thanks of all ranks has been sent to the Press at ENNISKILLEN. (cont'd)	

1577 Wt. W10791/1773 500,000 7/15 D. D. & L. A.D.S.S./Forms/C. 2118.

Army Form C. 2118.

WAR DIARY
or
INTELLIGENCE SUMMARY.
(Erase heading not required.)

Place	Date	Hour	Summary of Events and Information	Remarks and references to Appendices
TAMIE HON	22-12-15	6.30.	Mtd. Parade for Scheme in conjunction with 36th Cyclist Coy. Weather Wet.	Ref map AMIENS 1:80,000
	23-12-15	8-45	Horses exercised under Capt Hales. Distance covered this day 20 miles Weather fair	
	24-12-15	8-45	Horses exercised. Limeh dists[?] during afternoon. Weather Wet.	
	25-12-15		Christmas Day. C. of E. Holy Communion at 6.30 am. Parade Service at 9 am. A general holiday was observed this day. Men sat down to their dinner at 1pm and were visited by the C.O. & officers. The men seemed very pleased with the arrangements that had been made to serve a good dinner. In addition to the puddings from ENNISKILLEN, puddings were received from the DAILY NEWS.	
	26-12-15		C. of E. parade under Capt Hales at 10-15 am. Weather Stormy	
	27-12-15		Divine Day. Horses exercised at 9 am. Weather fine.	
	28-12-15	10.20	Mobilization Parade (Practice Scheme) just stores packed on wagons and supplies stored. 11-30 am - Horses exercised in full marching [?] & Watering.	
	29-12-15		Mtd. Parade for Scheme in conjunction with 36th Cyclist Coy. 2-15 pm. thunderstorm for a quarter of an hour. Weather Stormy.	

Army Form C. 2118.

WAR DIARY
or
INTELLIGENCE SUMMARY.
(Erase heading not required.)

Instructions regarding War Diaries and Intelligence Summaries are contained in F. S. Regs., Part II. and the Staff Manual respectively. Title pages will be prepared in manuscript.

Place	Date	Hour	Summary of Events and Information	Remarks and references to Appendices
FAMECHON	30-12-15	8am	Clean Billets	Refer map AMIENS 1:100,000
		6-9-	Physical Drill No 1, 2 Troops + Bayonet Exercise and Gas Helmets	
2		9.30	Physical Drill Bayonet Exercise and Gas Helmet" 10-0 Bombing. M Squadron Bombers at 9am. 2pm football hot baths for men. Weather fair.	
	31-12-15	8-00	M Parade in drill order for route march. The Squadron visited	
NEW YEAR'S EVE			CRÊCY. Capt Chamberlayne gave a brief history of the famous battle and pointed out the battlefield. Weather wet.	

A. Chamberlayne
Cmdg.
Service Sqdn. 6th. Dragoons

AT

1st S. Sp: 6th Suite: Spec:
Vol: 4

36

Army Form C. 2118.

WAR DIARY
~~INTELLIGENCE SUMMARY~~
(Erase heading not required.)

— CONFIDENTIAL —

WAR DIARY
of
Service Squadron 6th Inniskilling Dragoons

From 1st January 1916 To 31st January 1916

VOLUME IV

Kept by:- Arthur Capt
Service Squadron
6th Inniskilling Dragoons

Army Form C. 2118.

WAR DIARY
or
INTELLIGENCE SUMMARY.
(Erase heading not required.)

Instructions regarding War Diaries and Intelligence Summaries are contained in F. S. Regs., Part II. and the Staff Manual respectively. Title pages will be prepared in manuscript.

Place	Date	Hour	Summary of Events and Information	Remarks and references to Appendices
FAMECHON	1-1-16		New Year's Day. 9am to 11am Bayonet fighting with Gas Helmets & Physical Drill. Weather fine.	Ref Map AMIENS 1:80,000. Sheet 12
	2-1-16	8-40pm	C of E Parade for Divine Service. 9-30am Presbyterians & Wesleyans. Weather fine.	
	3-1-16	9 am	Squadron Parade in full marching Order with Transport. The Squadron will march under Capt Hicks to their Billets in new Area. Weather fine.	
St HILAIRE	4-1-16		The Squadron marched in yesterday & took over new Billets. The General state of the buildings was bad, and a great deal of work will have to be done to render the billets weatherproof. Horses of N° I & II Troops mallenied today. Weather fair.	Ref Map as above.
	5-1-16	9 am	General Fatigues. N° 3 & 4 Troops mallenied. Inspection of all horses by V.O. of those mallenied. Horses of N° 3 & 4 Troops mallenied.	
	6-1-16		Capt Hicks. 2pm Football. Weather fine.	
	7-1-16		Inspection of horses by V.O. General Fatigues & Exercising Horses. Weather fine.	
	8-1-16	8.30	Scheme in conjunction with 36th Cyclist Coy. The name of a place & troops observed not the weather or the kind of a communication whenever it is necessary to indicate to the address or address letters etc to the within this information should be mentioned in the text. Whenever it is necessary to write the name of any place when its write is not the most. Weather fine.	Ref Mil.P.O. No 13443

Army Form C. 2118.

WAR DIARY
or
INTELLIGENCE SUMMARY.
(Erase heading not required.)

Instructions regarding War Diaries and Intelligence Summaries are contained in F.S. Regs., Part II. and the Staff Manual respectively. Title pages will be prepared in manuscript.

Place	Date	Hour	Summary of Events and Information	Remarks and references to Appendices
St. HILAIRE	9-1-16	9-50am	C of E parade for Divine Service at DOMART. 2-30pm Presbyterians Wesleyans to Divine & Recreation Room at DOMART. S.O. Each man is entitled to one green envelope per week which will be issued to him with his pay. Weather fine.	Ref Map AMIENS 1-40,000 Sheet-12
	10-1-16		General fatigues & Returns to Billets. Evening stores. No. 203 Pt. G.W. McKeown rejoined the Squadron today. Offrs McKeown & McCullagh will proceed to the base. Nos 3-4 Troops Riding School at the Jumps. Weather fair.	
	11-1-16	9-30	Jumping for Troops 1-2. Reminders Exercise stores. Spur Musketry with Mark Helmets for 1-2 Troops. 3-4 Troops clean up return billets. Order published that no officer or soldier (in other person subject to military law) is permitted to be in possession of a camera. Order published that many cases have recently come to notice in which men proceeding on leave have taken with them unverified letters, in order that if at any time during their journey they are found in possession of unverified letters, they will be placed under arrest and sent back to their units. Weather fine.	Ref. M.O. No. 293
	12-1-16		Mtd Parade at 8am & 5pm. Spur Scraping for Squadron Carbines. Weather wet.	

1577 Wt. W10791/1773 500,000 1/15 D.D.&L. A.D.S.S./Forms/C. 2118.

Army Form C. 2118.

WAR DIARY
or
INTELLIGENCE SUMMARY.
(Erase heading not required.)

Place	Date	Hour	Summary of Events and Information	Remarks and references to Appendices
ST HILAIRE	13-1-16	9:45am	Dismounted Parade for route march without arms. 2:15pm Inspection of Lines Horses and Stable Equipment. Weather fine	Ref Maps AMIENS 1:50,000
"	14-1-16	6:45 a.m.	O.C. Parade for march to RAINCHEVAL (8 miles E+N6) Weather fine	Ref Maps AMIENS 1:50,000
"	15-1-16		Horse Parade at 11 a.m. for inspection by O.C. 2pm Sports- match Westshires	
"	16-1-16		No Divine service was held today for C of E. Wesleyans & Presbyterians at 10:45 a.m. Weather fair	
"	17-1-16	6:45am	Parade under troop leaders for Range Taking & judging distance. 2pm Foot drill for N.C.Os. 2-3-4 Troops staff Pastrol. N.C.Os. troop musketry. Weather fine	
"	18-1-16	6:45	Horses received under troop leaders 2pm N°3 troop musketry Westshires	
"	19-1-16	6:45	Horses received & judging distances under troop leaders 2pm foot drill under the I.S.M. for all N.C.Os. 2pm. Special A.R.O. N°13/61 the use of the green envelopes in multiple letters is intended to enable men friends more than one letter of a private nature which they may not wish to submit to censorship within sack of his Troop Commander. They are only to contain letters from the person whose signature the certificate on the cover supports. & without more than one condition in possession	A.R.O. N°13/61
			Weather Wet	

Army Form C. 2118.

WAR DIARY
or
INTELLIGENCE SUMMARY.
(Erase heading not required.)

Instructions regarding War Diaries and Intelligence Summaries are contained in F. S. Regs., Part II. and the Staff Manual respectively. Title pages will be prepared in manuscript.

Place	Date	Hour	Summary of Events and Information	Remarks and references to Appendices
ST HILAIRE	20-1-16	8.0am	Reconnaissance Scheme from St HILAIRE PT 135. Weather fine	
	21-1-16	9.15am	Scheme of Conjunction with 36th Cyclist Coy. The 14th Corps Commander witnessed the operation and was accompanied by the 36th Divisional Commander. Operation ceased at LE MEILLARD. Ref map AMIENS 1: 80,000. Weather fine	Ref map AMIENS 1:80,000
	22-1-16	4pm	Mr Carrick under C.O. Carpenter Mr Brande under S.S.M. 2pm Inspection of Equipment by C.O. Weather wet.	
	23-1-16	8am	Divine Service Parade under Capt Mathew for service at BERNEUIL at 9-45am. In Church the Authority of Army's monument the service. Weather fine Speedometer No. 422. Section literature. Pamphlet by Jens Addams on being circulated to the troops. Specimen of this pamphlet is secured and to be sent to the Orderly Room.	Ref map AMIENS 1:80,000
	24-1-16	8.0	Parade at 8.0 for Divisional Scheme as per secret instructions. Weather fine	
	25-1-16	8.45	Musketry by Section Semaphore. 2pm Inspection of Saddlery. Weather fine	
	26-1-16		Parade handed for Divisional Scheme as per secret instructions. 2/Lieuts Mathew, McWilliam, Sergt. Cairns, the Sergt. Reid proceed to the Divl Schools of Instruction at LE MEILLARD. (Ref map AMIENS 1:80,000). Weather fine	Att

WAR DIARY

Army Form C. 2118.

Instructions regarding War Diaries and Intelligence Summaries are contained in F.S. Regs., Part II. and the Staff Manual respectively. Title pages will be prepared in manuscript.

(Erase heading not required.)

Place	Date	Hour	Summary of Events and Information	Remarks and references to Appendices
ST. HILAIRE	27-1-16	9-30	General fatigues in cleaning up billets. 9-45-11-45 Musketry. Atmosphere Bayonet-fighting. From Rifle Inspection. Weather fine.	B.H. Maps AMIENS 1.80,000
	28-1-16		Squadron paraded to take part in Divisional Tactical Exercise. Weather fine.	
	29-1-16	9 am	Foot drill for all N.C.O.'s – men. 12 noon Horse Inspection by this same reporting for Squadron Equipment. Weather fine.	
	30-1-16	9-45	Divine Service Parade at BERNEUIL for C. of E. Weather fine.	
	31-1-16		Capt. Chamberlayne proceeded on leave to England & Capt Hicks assumed command of the Squadron. Capt. Chamberlayne gazetted as Temp. Major whilst commanding the Annex Squadron. 6th Inns'k' Dragoons. 6-30 Horses exercised. Signalling Squadron Signallers the near party of FAMECHON having completed their Antics rejoined the Squadron today. Weather fine.	

A.H.H... Cmdg.
Service Sqdn. 6th. Dragoons.

SERIAL NO. 73.

Confidential

War Diary

of

Service Squadron, 6th Inniskilling Dragoons.

FROM 1st February 1916 TO 31st March 1916.

Army Form C. 2118.

WAR DIARY
~~of~~
~~INTELLIGENCE SUMMARY.~~
(Erase heading not required.)

CONFIDENTIAL
WAR DIARY
of
Service Squadron 6th Inniskilling Dragoons
From 1st February 1916 To 29th February 1916
VOLUME V

Army Form C. 2118.

WAR DIARY
or
INTELLIGENCE SUMMARY.
(Erase heading not required.)

Instructions regarding War Diaries and Intelligence Summaries are contained in F. S. Regs., Part II. and the Staff Manual respectively. Title pages will be prepared in manuscript.

Place	Date	Hour	Summary of Events and Information	Remarks and references to Appendices
ST HILAIRE LAVICOGNE	9 Feb. 22 Feb		February — The Squadron moved from HILLS to LAVICOGNE. On this date the Squadron marched to YAUCHELLES-LES-AUTHIE and billeted, moving on to BERTRANCOURT later. During the month the Squadron was employed on various duties such as orderlies to DIV. HD. QRTS and police work on road control. A motor machine gun battery was killed with us. The Squadron continued its training when weather permitted. Weather during month was bad much snow having fallen. Leave being open certain Officers. N.C.O's then proceeded to their homes on furlough.	Br Muf AMIENS 12 Feb 08

A Chamberlayne Capt Cmdg.
Service Sqdn. 6th (Dragoons.)

Army Form C. 2118.

WAR DIARY
or
INTELLIGENCE SUMMARY.
(Erase heading not required.)

Confidential

War Diary

of

Service Squadron 6th Inniskilling Dragoons

From 1st March 1916 To 31st March 1916

Volume VI

Kept by A/Lt Brinsmead

Army Form C. 2118.

WAR DIARY
~~INTELLIGENCE SUMMARY~~
(Erase heading not required.)

Place	Date	Hour	Summary of Events and Information	Remarks and references to Appendices
VAUCHELLES	4"	9 A.M.	— March — Under orders received the Squadron moved this day to new billets at BERTRANCOURT. Although only a short distance to cover men and horses felt fatigued on arrival the march having taken place in a snowstorm. Men and horses were well billeted in the town and very comfortable. Hot baths were arranged. Although training soon carried out it was only until difficulty owing to numbers of roads debarred to such troops and crops in the vicinity. Except in a few days the weather on the whole was good.	New Maps AMIENS 1/2 80,000
BERTRANCOURT			Whilst at BERTRANCOURT we witnessed a great deal of air reconnaissance and the daily flights of British and Enemy aeroplanes.	

A. Chamberlayne Major Cmdg.
Service Sqdn. 6th Dragoons.

SERIAL NO. 1/3.

Confidential
War Diary

of

XXXVI ULSTER DIVⁿ

6ᵗʰ Inniskilling Dragoons. (Service Squadron)

FROM 1ˢᵗ March 1916 TO 31ˢᵗ March 1916.

Volume 6

Army Form C. 2118.

WAR DIARY
or
INTELLIGENCE SUMMARY.

(Erase heading not required.)

CONFIDENTIAL

WAR DIARY
of
SERVICE SQUADRON 6th INNISKILLING DRAGOONS

From 1st March 1916 To 31st March 1916

VOLUME VI

Kept by Lieutenant Colonel
Service Squadron
6th Inniskilling Dragoons

Army Form C. 2118.

WAR DIARY
INTELLIGENCE SUMMARY.
(Erase heading not required.)

Instructions regarding War Diaries and Intelligence Summaries are contained in F. S. Regs., Part II. and the Staff Manual respectively. Title pages will be prepared in manuscript.

Place	Date	Hour	Summary of Events and Information	Remarks and references to Appendices
VACHELLES	1.3.16		8 men who joined the Sqdn as a reinforcement from 2nd Reserve Cavalry Regt ALDERSHOT	ALDERSHOT Ref. AM1E M3 Sheet 12- 1.80,000
LA VICOGNE			paraded for map reading under C.B. Snowfall.	
BERTRANCOURT	3.3.16		Squadron billeted here. Wet & cold	
VACHELLES to AOTHIE	4.3.16	10 am		
"	5.3.16		Severe snowstorm.	
"	6.3.16		5 a/Cpl Keyes proceeded to 36th Divl Anti Gas school for instruction. Snowstorm.	
"	8.3.16		Severe frost. 4 Sqdn on bicycles inspected. Lce/Sergt Reed sent to O.C.	
"	9.3.16		36th Divl Train at LEALVILLERS to look after 20 water carts with punand + hasso	
"	13.3.16		No 182 Pte Allen J. attended improved act 2 a/Cpl Lee	
"	14.3.16		Inspection of horses, collars & horse rubbers.	
"	15.3.16		Sergt Huffill & Cpl Davies detailed to attend 3rd Course at the 36th Divl School of Instruction at BERNAVAL on 20th inst.	
"	17.3.16		St Patrick's day Sqdn beaten 3 goals to 2 by 109th Field Ambulance at Football	
"	18.3.16		La/Cpl Keyes gave good lecture on Anti-Gas to the Sqdn here.	

Army Form C. 2118.

WAR DIARY
or
INTELLIGENCE SUMMARY.

(Erase heading not required.)

Instructions regarding War Diaries and Intelligence Summaries are contained in F. S. Regs., Part II. and the Staff Manual respectively. Title pages will be prepared in manuscript.

Place	Date	Hour	Summary of Events and Information	Remarks and references to Appendices
BERTRAM COBRT.	18.3.16		20 men sent to C.R.E. for Tree Felling - 20 men sent to Town Commandant for road cleaning	
"	19.3.16		No 249 Pte McCabe awarded 14 days F.P.No I for not complying with an order -	
"	20.3.16	7.a.m	Horse rugs inspected - 2 men of 1st Royal Irish Rifles attached MAILLY-MAILLET. Squadron for Destruction. Squadron marched another eyesight. L/Sergt Reed promoted Sergt. Corpl Davis promoted L/Sergt	
"	21.3.16	10 a.m	supplied 10 men to Crichmer Dump ACHEUX. 1 NCO 7 men sent to 32nd Dragoons DERNACOBRT for loading stores.	
"	22.3.16		Hay Pile inspected. No 11g L/Corpl Hamilton detailed to attend Course of Instruction at S^to OMAR on HOTCHKISS gun	
"	23.3.16	8.30am	Despatch Riding Scheme to	
"	25.3.16		No 223 L/Corpl Irons deprived of Paid Le stripe	

A Chamberlayne Major
Cmdg.
Service Sqdn. 6th Dragoons.

SERIAL NO. 73.

XXXV

Confidential

War Diary

to

Service Squadron, 6th Inniskilling Dragoons

FROM 1st April 1916 TO 30th April 1916.

WAR DIARY

INTELLIGENCE SUMMARY.

(Erase heading not required.)

Army Form C. 2118.

CONFIDENTIAL

WAR DIARY

of

SERVICE SQUADRON 6th INNISKILLING DRAGOONS

From 1st April 1916 To 30th April 1916

VOLUME VII

Army Form C. 2118.

WAR DIARY

INTELLIGENCE SUMMARY.

(Erase heading not required.)

Instructions regarding War Diaries and Intelligence Summaries are contained in F. S. Regs., Part II. and the Staff Manual respectively. Title pages will be prepared in manuscript.

Place	Date	Hour	Summary of Events and Information	Remarks and references to Appendices
CONTAY	1.4.16 - 4.4.16		Weather like Summer. Engaged on reconnaissance of 36th Divisional area endeavouring to find ground for bivouac camps. Practically whole area 30 square miles crops of under plough.	Ref AMIENS 1 map 12.
"	4.4.16		20 III Troop 2 Officers billets changed to allow 96th Infy Brigade 32nd Division to move in. CONTAY is not in 36th Divisional area but 32nd Division.	
St OUEN.	7.4.16	5 pm	Moved here on way to join Meerut Cavalry Brigade for training 13th - 26th inst. 36th Ind Cyclist Company also join in training. Shelters coats, vests, gloves, one man blanket & haversacks sent into Ordnance. All Horses picketed out. Men one Blanket, horse saddle blanket, night's cold.	
St RIQUIER	13.4.16	11.30 am	Attached to Meerut Cavalry Bde for Training. Brigadier Genl Edwards 13th Hussars. 3rd Skinners Horse - 18th Lancers and Brigade.	
MARTAINNE VILLE	20.4.16	1 pm	Marched with Meerut Bde as far as MOYENVILLE then branched off with 36th Cyclist Bat Company.	ABBEVILLE 2 map 11
			Sunday April 16th HOC sent the squadron + cyclists to do an advance guard scheme from Trust - West to a Tactical Exercise was carried out with the Bde. The Squadron + Cyclist Company are billeted here till the 26th being able attacked	

1577 Wt. W10791/1773 500,000 1/15 D. D. & L. A.D.S.S./Forms/C. 2118.

Army Form C. 2118.

WAR DIARY
or
INTELLIGENCE SUMMARY.

(Erase heading not required.)

Instructions regarding War Diaries and Intelligence Summaries are contained in F.S. Regs., Part II. and the Staff Manual respectively. Title pages will be prepared in manuscript.

Place	Date	Hour	Summary of Events and Information	Remarks and references to Appendices
	April			
MARTAINNEVILLE	21st		to present Colo for training. Headquarters of which are now AIGNEVILLE. Good Friday. Poured with rain all day.	
	22nd		Sqdn + Cyclist Officers Instruction under Col Grimston 18th Lancers abandoned owing to wet.	
	24		Convoy scheme (Sqdns Cyclists) Genl Edwards Chief Empire Brigade Staff rode	
	25		Billeted for the night with Lancashire Hussar Sqdn + 30th Cyclist Company.	
HANGEST sur SOMME	26			
	27		Leave again open 4 vacancies for 30th every 5 days. Am now again in 36th Divisional Area.	
PUCHEVILLERS	28	1 pm		

A Chamberlayne Major
O in C
Service Sqdn. 6th Dragoons.

36 Div 6 Inns Drag

Vol 7

WAR DIARY
Army Form C. 2118.

~~INTELLIGENCE SUMMARY.~~
(Erase heading not required.)

Instructions regarding War Diaries and Intelligence Summaries are contained in F. S. Regs., Part II. and the Staff Manual respectively. Title pages will be prepared in manuscript.

Confidential
War Diary
of 6th Inniskilling Dragoons
Service Squadron
From 1st May 1916 To 31st May 1916
Volume VIII

kept by A Chamberlayne
Major
Service Sqdn. 6th. Dragoons.

WAR DIARY

INTELLIGENCE SUMMARY.

Army Form C. 2118.

Place	Date	Hour	Summary of Events and Information	Remarks and references to Appendices
PUCHVILLERS.	May 1st		2nd Lieut. Mac William was detailed to instruct 12 men in the use of the Hotchkiss gun, he having recently been through a short course at St OMAR.	
	May 2nd	7.15am	A/Cpl Perry 38 and 14 Sawers 1039 Battn went to 36th Divl Signal Coy for a course of Visual Signalling.	
			During the month 4 parties were sent up to the trenches for 3 days at a time to make themselves acquainted with the country held by the enemy in front of them.	
			The weather during the month was gloriously fine.	
			For some weeks Antrim dully went to bathe at BAVELINCOURT but this was afterwards forbidden by the Higher Authorities.	
			Three men every 5 days were allowed on leave to the United Kingdom. 8 days to England & 9 days to Ireland.	
			A Party of 30 men daily was supplied unloading ammunition at PUCHVILLERS. Remaining men exercise etc Kress- railhead.- Foster for 32nd Division were also supplied.	
	29th		Detachment went to Rifle Range at MILLENCOURT for ranyi Practice with Hotchkiss Gun- New Hotchkiss gun arrived.	

WAR DIARY

INTELLIGENCE SUMMARY

Army Form C. 2118.

Place	Date	Hour	Summary of Events and Information	Remarks and references to Appendices
	May 30		Received instructions that Squadron would sail with 2 squadrons of the 10th Irish Horse form the 10th Corps Cavalry Regt. The organization will be 1 Offr & 6 clerks as Corps Mounted Troops. Divisional Cavalry no longer exists. — Sergt Turner left to join the 7th Cadet Corps in Ireland with a view of obtaining a commission.	

C. Chamberlayne Major
Cmdg.
Service Sqdn. 6th. Dragoons.

www.ingramcontent.com/pod-product-compliance
Lightning Source LLC
Chambersburg PA
CBHW081247170426
43191CB00037B/2074